Romanesque

Romanesque

PEEBLES ART LIBRARY   **Sandy Lesberg, Editor**

First published 1974
by
Peebles Press International.
U.S.: 140 Riverside Drive, New York, N.Y. 10024
U.K.: 12 Thayer Street, London, W1M 5LD

ISBN 0-85690-034-6

All the illustrations were provided by
André Held, Lausanne
except from Giraudon, Paris: page 29.

Distributed by
Walden Books, Resale Division in the
U.S. and Canada.
WHS Distributors in the U.K., Ireland,
Australia, New Zealand and South Africa.

Printed and Bound in Great Britain

Introduction

The creative force of the artists in the 11th and 12th centuries gave birth to a style which spread over all that Western civilisation which derived from Charlemagne's Empire, and left its mark on every branch of art. It is seen in architecture, sculpture, ivories, textiles, goldsmiths' work, and painting in various forms, such as illuminated manuscripts, mural paintings and stained glass. Many affinities can be seen in this Romanesque period between the various styles of these arts, a similarity between a sculptured figure and an illuminated manuscript, or between the motif of a piece of goldsmiths' work and the theme of a fresco. The reliquary at Conques-en-Rouergue, for instance, and a Christ in Majesty of the 12th century painted in an apse of a church are proof of this. Often the decorative theme is the same; for instance, where the meander pattern, interspersed with scrolls, in which appear paintings of animals, reappears in the murals of the Baptistry of St. Jean de Poitiers; or in the frieze of the tympanum at Carennac (Lot); or again, when it is used as a frame to the miniature in a manuscript at Cîteaux. These three works date from the beginning of the 12th century.

Nevertheless, the two arts most closely linked are the arts of illumination and wall painting; here the resemblances are evident in many ways.

Some people assert that priority must be given to the art of illumination over that of mural painting; but the premises on which they base their argument appear false. Very probably, currents of influence flowed both ways; illuminations served as models for frescoes and, reciprocally, frescoes were sources of inspiration for illuminations. And sometimes, certainly in the great abbeys, the monks who copied and decorated the manuscripts in the scriptoria, *may well have been the same men who, on the orders of the Abbot or Chapter, mounted on scaffolding and covered the walls of the church or refectory with painted scenes. In the case of Romanesque stained glass, we have little contemporary evidence; but it is worth recalling the programme dictated by Suger for the Abbey church of St. Denis in the middle of the 12th century.*

It is at least reasonable to assume that the art of illumination contributed more to mural painting than it received. Manuscripts are certainly more portable, and can circulate freely, even over great distances, and by devious routes; whereas by its nature, mural painting is a fixture. Probably, it is thanks to manuscripts rather than to travelling artists from Byzantium itself, that Byzantine influence is seen in the paintings in the north gallery of the Cathedral of Le Puy (Haute-Loire), from the end of the 11th century.

Whatever may be said, it is fair to assume that the catalogue of Western illuminated manuscripts and mural paintings of the Romanesque period is virtually complete, with the exception, however, of future discoveries of frescoes covered by overpainting or plaster of more recent date; these may be of great value.

A subject hitherto relatively ignored deserves attention; the comparison of illuminated manuscripts and mural paintings of the Romanesque period; for although, up to now, the affinity between these two forms of art has been established, their study was for the most part undertaken separately. By examining this subject and going back to their origins, the prototypes common to the old Romanesque themes can perhaps be identified; and the painted decoration both of illuminated manuscripts and church walls can be shown to have enriched more than any other art the iconography of the 11th and 12th centuries. For, compared with sculpture in stone, goldsmiths' or ivory work, painting is relatively inexpensive and quickly executed. No comparison can be made between the time taken to decorate the most exuberant page of an illuminated manuscript, or even to fresco a wall of several square metres, representing a scene with figures, and that taken by a sculptor to finish the smallest bas-relief in stone, or by a goldsmith to make a reliquary, or by a worker in ivory to carve the binding of a missal.

The consequence was that the most complete cycles known to us are those of painting, and in this way a greater knowledge is gained of the Romanesque period; and yet we possess only very little evidence of what the art of the 11th and 12th century fresco painters was, and of how many manuscripts written and decorated at that time have disappeared. The remaining material is but a pale reflection of what once existed.

Painting must be credited with another advantage. The invasions of the barbarians from the 5th to the 10th centuries did not arrest its advance, as they did that of stone sculpture. For evidence we need only think of the great mass of mural paintings still intact at Tarrasa in Spain (6th century), at Castelseprio in Italy (7th century?), at Müstair in Switzerland (beginning of the 9th century), at St. Germain of Auxerre in France (middle of the 9th century), at Oberzell in Germany near Lake Constance (10th century): as well as the many illuminated manuscripts, Carolingian and Ottonian, which form the chief glory of certain libraries.

A good claim can be made that the golden age of illumination, even more of mural painting, was the Romanesque period. By employing a certain formalised style, notably the simplicity and strength of the outline, the flat tint of pure colours, the backgrounds without depth, by avoiding the use of graduated shadows, the artists of those days endowed their work with great strength. The same can be said for the art of stained glass—as long as it employed the mosaic principle.

In the same way that a Romanesque fresco sinks into the plaster it covers, an illumination of the same period takes complete possession of the page it decorates. This explains why Romanesque art is today again regarded as important.

Marc Thibout
Curator of the Musée
des monuments français.

Egbert's Psalter. School of Reichenau
" The monk Ruodprecht presenting his work "
10th century
Cividale del Friuli, Archaeological Museum

Fresco in the crypt
David (?) felling the lion (detail)
12th century
Church of Tavant

Christ mounted on a white horse
placed in the centre of a Cross encrusted
with jewels. Placed in the four intersections
of the cross are the four celestial horsemen
12th century
Auxerre Cathedral

St. John and the Virgin
Detail from an altar frontal
Valltarga (Cerdagne)
Beginning of 13th century
Barcelona, Museum of Catalan Art

English Manuscript
Psalterium cum canticis
" St. Eustace "
13th century
Venice, Marciana Library

Scene from the legend of St. Eustace
Apparition of Christ between the horns of a stag.
About 1205-1210
Dreuse, church of St. Peter

Scene from the legend of St. Eustace
Departure into exile of St. Eustace and his family
About 1205-1210
Dreuse, church of St. Peter

Gospel Book of Vysehrad
"The Baptism of Christ". About 1085
Prague, National and University Library

Mark and the Evangelists' symbols
8th century
St. Gall, Convent Library

Annunciation and Visitation
Fragment of Mural Decoration
Detail of the Visitation
Catalonia about 1200
Puigreig, parish church of

Principal events in the lives of the
Archangels St. Michael and St. Gabriel
From Eguillor (Navarre)
13th century
Barcelona, Museum of Catalan Art

Frescoes from the vault
of the Pantheon of Kings
Annunciation to the Shepherds (detail)
12th century
Leon, San Isidoro

School of Canterbury
St. Augustine de Civitate Dei
11th century
Florence, Laurentian Library

Christ in Majesty surrounded
by the twelve apostles
and four saints
Lower section: a saint
12th century
Church of Berzé-la-Ville

French School
The Bible of Cîteaux
"King David"
12th century
Dijon, Municipal Library

French Manuscript
Life of St. Amand
Scenes from the life of the saint
Middle of the 12th century
Valenciennes Library

Fresco of the triumphal arch
Calendar: *September*
Laval (Mayenne) church of Pritz

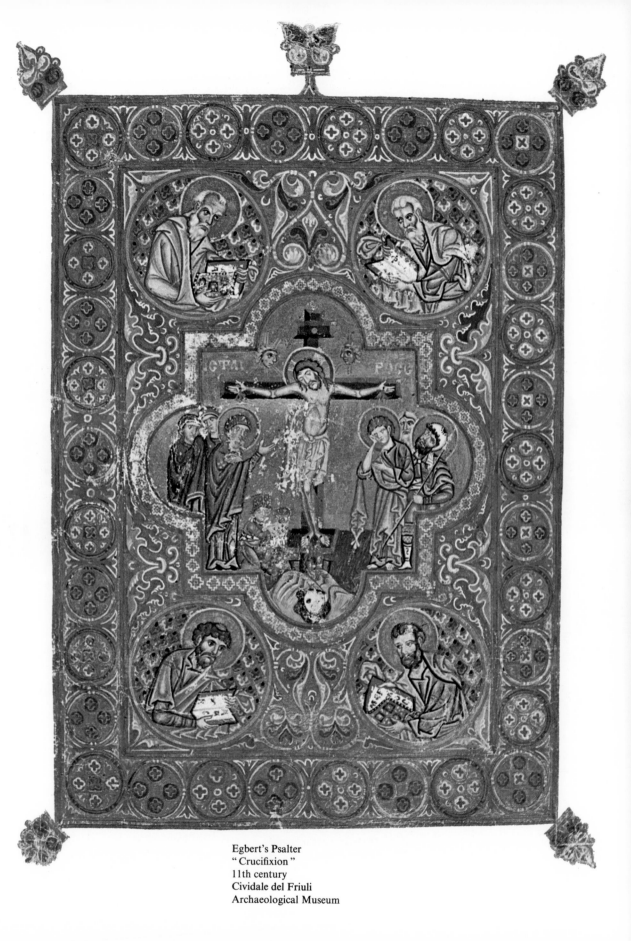

Egbert's Psalter
" Crucifixion "
11th century
Cividale del Friuli
Archaeological Museum

Frescoes in the Oratory of St. Sylvester
The legates of Constantine
and the hermit St. Sylvester
13th century
Rome, convent of Santi Quattro Coronati

Scenes from the Martyrdom of St. Juliet
and St. Quirico from the Hermitage
of St. Juliet of Durro (valley of Bohi)
Altar frontal. 12th century
Barcelona, Museum of Catalan Art

Life and Martyrdom of St. Savin and of St. Cyprien
Martyrdom of both saints (detail)
End of the 11th century
Church of St. Savin-sur-Gartempe

The Virgin and Child enthroned, surrounded
by scenes from the Passion of St. Margaret
Second half of the 12th century
Vich, Episcopal Museum

Life and Martyrdom of St. Savin and St. Cyprien
St. Savin and St. Cyprien in front of Maximum
(detail)
End of the 11th century
Church of St. Savin-sur-Gartempe

Calendar: *May*
End of 12th century
Church of Vieux-Pouzauges
(Vendée)

The Childhood of Christ (detail)
12th century window
Chartres Cathedral

Virgin in Majesty with apostles
Auvergne, church of Lavaudieu

Christ and the Virgin from a *Tree of Jesse*
From the Abbey of Jarcy or Gercy (Aisne)
About 1205-1210
Paris, Louvre

Head of Christ
From Wissembourg
11th century

Christ on the Cross and scenes from the Passion
The kiss of Judas (detail)
School of Pisa, second half of 12th century
Florence, Uffizi Gallery

Pantocrator and the Last Supper
12th century
Trôo (Loir-et-Cher)
Church of St. Jacques-des-Guérets

Adoration of the Magi
Church of St. Fargeau (Yonne)
13th century or beginning of 14th century
Geneva Museum, from the Ariana Museum

*Victory of the Archangel Michael over the
Apocalyptic Dragon*
First half of the 12th century
Civate, church of San Pietro al Monte

Romanesque manuscript. Mozarabic school
Beatus, *Commentary on the Apocalypse*
Turin, National Library

Corripe me domine, verum
tamen in iudicio, et no
in furore tuo, ne
forte ad nihiluz re
digas me.

Elijah on the Chariot of Fire
About 1255
Anagni, crypt of the Cathedral

The Ages of Man or the man microcosm
About 1255
Anagni, crypt of the Cathedral

Beatus, *Commentary on the Apocalypse*
"Bird killing a serpent"
Mozarabic school. 975
Gerona, Chapter House Library

Zacharius writing
St. Gabriel's chapel, 12th century
Canterbury Cathedral

The Virgin between the Prophets
The Magi Balthazar and Melchior (detail)
First half of 13th century
Vich, Episcopal Museum

Martyrdom of St. Vincent
From the basilica of St. Denis
About 1145
Paris, National Monuments Collection

Christ in Majesty
Archangel St. Michael (detail)
About 1007
Basilica of San Vincenzo at Galliano

The Crucifixion of St. Peter and the
Decapitation of St. Paul
1150-1170
Abbey church of Müstair (Engadine)

Six panels from the 153 which make a ceiling
The Washing of the Feet, The Last Supper,
The Arrest (Judas' kiss), *The Arrest* (Soldiers),
St. Martin and St. Hilary, The Raising
of a Dead Man
Middle of the 12th century
Church of Zillis (Grisons)

Christ on Cross with the sun and the moon,
the Virgin and St. John
12th century
Trôo (Loir-et-Cher)
Church of St. Jacques-des-Guérets

Frescoes from San Quirce of Pe⟨
Eucharist scene, 12th century
Solsona, Diocesan Museum

Beatus. *Commentary of the Apocalypse*
"The opening of the Seventh Seal"
Mozarabic school. 975
Gerona, Chapter House Library

Glossary of Romanesque Art

Alcuin (about 738-804)

(Albinus Flaccus.) A religious scholar born in the province of York. A pupil of the Venerable Bede and Egbert, he was schooled at York. He met Charlemagne in Italy, and remained with him. Alcuin was one of the principal collaborators in Charlemagne's scholarly work, the man really responsible for the revival of the letters and sciences of the Gauls. He was head of the palace school of Aix-la-Chapelle and that of Tours. He wrote scholarly manuals, and fought the heresiarchs, Felix of Urgel and Elipand of Toledo. He was a member of the Palatine Academy and took the pseudonym of Flaccus. His most celebrated work is the *Confession of Faith*.

Anagni

The painter who decorated the two vaults of Anagni Cathedral in Italy was one of the greatest Italo-Byzantine masters. In one vault he depicted a magnificent figure of Christ (the bust) in the centre of four scenes derived from the story of Samuel, and in the other the battle of Maspht. The crypt contains an even more important collection by the same artist. He painted some philosophical and scientific subjects; the four ages of man, the four temperaments, the elements, the creation of man, medicine represented by Galen and Hippocrates, etc. But the main decorative work is a series of episodes from the stories of the Ark of the Covenant, of Saul, Samuel and the book of the Apocalypse. There are also a number of figures of saints. These frescoes are of great aesthetic merit. The figures are solemn and majestic with graceful lines and of rich and varied hues. The impression of movement is remarkable. The clothes draped in a conventional manner, and the rather stereotyped faces reveal Byzantine influence; but the rigidity and oriental harshness of expression have disappeared. These frescoes are dated about 1255.

Andernach (Germany)

The church of Our Lady was started at the end of the 12th century. The main building was finished in 1212. The decoration dates from the first half of the 13th century and it is probable that the *Crucifixion* is even later. It is in the South Chapel. Under the cross, the bust of a nude and bearded man is shown, whose arms are raised to heaven. This represents Adam. Between the two windows is a *Virgin and St. John*, and to the right, an isolated figure with a halo and an angel overhead.

Angers (France)

The *Cathedral*. Hugues de Semblançay decorated all the windows of the nave with stained glass before 1149. Most of these works have disappeared, and those that remain have been much restored, except for the *Passion of Saint Catherine of Alexandria* (six medallions), which are on the left side of the nave. These works show how advanced the art of painting on glass was in the 12th century. *The St. Aubin Cloister* (now part of the *préfecture*) has a curious arch at the entrance of the old chapter house. It is decorated with both sculptures and paintings.

Aosta (Valley of)

The collegiate church of San Pietro ed Orso

at Aosta, in Italy, has an important series of frescoes, dating from the beginning of the 12th century; they illustrate the lives of the apostles. Above a decorative frieze (Greek key pattern interspersed with birds), it is still possible to see fragments of these works, particularly St. Andrew rowing the boat during the storm on the Lake of Galilee, and the martyrdom of St. James the Great. The figures are full of expression and painted with an almost brutal force. These paintings resemble those on the lateral walls of San Vincenzo at Galliano.

Argolell (Catalonia)

From the decoration in the apse of Argolell all that remains (in the Barcelona Museum) is the Virgin holding the chalice of the Holy Grail and five apostles, among whom St. Paul, St. John and St. Philip are remarkable. St. Paul holds an open book with a legend relating to the chosen vessel. The master of Argolell was influenced by the master of Pedret. He is a sensitive painter whose figures have gravity and naturalness; he achieves a great effect using only a limited range of colour.

Augsburg (Germany)

The five big figures which decorate the windows of the Augsburg Cathedral in Germany date from the beginning of the 12th century. The backgrounds, as often in stained glass windows of that period in Germany, are not coloured. They are among the oldest examples of painting on glass which have come down to us.

Auxerre (France)

Abbey of *St. Germain*. The frescoes in the crypt are some of the oldest in France. They date from the Carolingian period and were executed about 855 during the reign of Charles the Bald. Apart from a painted decoration (false columns, false capitals, ornamental vegetation), there are still three scenes with figures: St. Stephen preaching; the saint being accused by the Jews; his stoning. The design is very simple, but the workmanship is powerful, and the composition elegant. To the east, on the walls of the "confessio", two Bishops of Auxerre are depicted with the same precision and sobriety of colour.

Cathedral: The crypt is decorated with an unusual scene: Christ in the centre of a cross encrusted with jewels, surrounded by four horsemen placed in circular medallions. This is a subject taken from the Apocalypse. The painting appears to date from the end of the 11th century, but the faces must have been retouched in Gothic times.

Barbera (Catalonia)

In the church of Santa Maria the decoration of the two apsidal chapels remains *in situ*. On the pulpit side is *Christ between St. Peter and St. Paul*, *The Presentation of the Keys to St. Peter*, *The Crucifixion of St. Peter*, in front of a bishop and two women bringing offerings, and *The Beheading of St. Paul*. The chapel on the north side has paintings illustrating the story of the True Cross: the *Exaltation by Constantine and St. Helen*, the *Adoration of the two Angels* and the *Miracle of the Resurrection of a Youth* (due to touching the wood of the cross when it was found). The palette, which is rich in grey mixed with blue, carmine and a very transparent green, as well as the style, points to this being the work of the master of Polinya. The paintings in the central apse were executed by another painter; they are later (beginning of the 13th century) and not nearly so interesting. They have none of the usual decorative horizontal bands, and the scenes are arranged in an arbitrary fashion which is far removed from the method employed in typically Romanesque paintings.

Berlanga (Spain)

The frescoes of the Hermitage of San Bandelio of Berlanga (Burgos) are now in the United States, in the Boston Museum and private collections. The upper part of the walls was decorated with scenes from the life of Christ, and we recognise the hand of the master who decorated the apse of Santa Maria of Tahull. The paintings on the lower part of these walls are even more interesting. They were no doubt done by a Hispano-Arab artist, and depict a hare and a stag hunt, exotic animals, bears, dromedaries, elephants and medallions ornamented with oriental motifs. These frescoes reproduce examples of Mozarabic painting in the 10th century.

Berzé-la-Ville (Burgundy)

The Abbot St. Hugh who was head of the Order of Cluny from 1049 to 1109, often came in search of rest to a small isolated priory among the vines. He had had it built and decorated at the same time as the church of Cluny. A collection of paintings has been well preserved in the apse of the upper chapel, dating from the beginning of the 12th century. In the semi-dome of the apse appears a *Christ in Majesty* (3 metres 90 cms. in height) surrounded by the twelve apostles and four saints. The lower parts of the apse are decorated with six figures of saints. At the base are the busts of saints who were particularly venerated by the order of Cluny. In the left arcade, an episode in the legend of St. Blaise is illustrated (the saint making a wolf give back a pig to a poor old woman from whom it had taken it); also his martyrdom. In the right arcade: *The Martyrdom of St. Lawrence* in the presence of the prefect Dacian. At the entrance of the choir are two standing figures wearing hoods and holding crooks. Presumably they are effigies of the first Abbots of Cluny. Above them is ornamental foliage coming out of amphoras—a traditional oriental decorative motif. From the paintings which decorated the nave only a few traces remain; on the west wall, *The Entry of Christ into Jerusalem*.

Besse-en-Chandesse (Auvergne)

In the parish of St. Pierre-Colamine (Puy-de-Dôme), near Besse-en-Chandesse, are the Jonas grottoes decorated with paintings. These grottoes were a part of a fortress belonging to the Knights Templars. Frescoes in the chapel: above the entrance a *Virgin in Majesty holding the Child;* on the right of the entrance: *The Appearance of Christ to Mary Magdalene; The Holy Women at the Tomb*; to the left: *The Crown of Thorns, Jerusalem, The Arrest of Christ*. The latter scene is partly hidden by a supporting wall, as is the *Descent from the Cross* in which only the extremity of the cross is visible; above, the moon is depicted and beneath *Nicodemus extracting the Nail from the Hand of Christ*, while Joseph of Arimathea supports the arm. On the corner-stones of the arches in the nave are figures of prophets. These paintings, which probably date from the 11th century, are rough in execution. They recall Carolingian art. They also prove that Celtic influence long remained alive in the Auvergne.

Bourges (France)

This Cathedral, which is so famous for its Gothic stained glass, possesses a few panels which date from the 12th century in the outer aisle of the nave. They depict *The Annunciation, The Adoration of the Magi, The Rest at Simon's House, The Raising of Lazarus*. Although late in style, they still have an undeniably Romanesque character.

Burgal (Catalonia)

The apsidal decoration of the Benedictine monastery church of San Pedro is now in the Barcelona Museum. Fragments of a Pantocrator and the figure of a prophet in adoration are all that remain of the vault frescoes. The lower part of the Archangel Gabriel, who holds the traditional scroll with the word *POSTULACIUS*, is also visible. In the hemispherical section of the apse, which has three windows, are paintings of *The Virgin holding the Chalice of the Holy Grail*, *St. Peter holding the Keys* and *St. John the Baptist with the Lamb* shown in a circle placed on his knees. They are all seated on a bench running the whole length of the fresco. From the frieze which limits the lower drapery and is composed of sinuous lines interspersed with jewelled crowns, stands out the figure of the benefactress, the Countess of Pallars, holding a candle. Her donation in 1196 made it possible to paint this apse. The paintings are the work of the master of Pedret.

Canterbury

The crypt chapel known as the St. Gabriel Chapel. In the intrados of a niche: seven stars in a medallion, St. John writing the Apocalypse, and seven angels praying or holding candlesticks. On the vault of the chancel: the Pantocrator blessing, placed in the centre of a mandorla supported by four angels. On the north wall: scenes from the history of St. John the Baptist. On the south wall: *The Annunciation*, *The Visitation* and *The Birth of Christ*. In certain parts are seraphim holding scrolls, or accompanied by wheels of fire. These frescoes show Byzantine influence and date from the middle of the 12th century. The Chapel of St. Anselm. The only remaining decoration is a remarkable painting which has a distinct affinity with the Winchester illuminations: *St. Paul and the Viper* (end of 12th century). Preserved in the same Cathedral are fine windows, dating from the end of the 12th or the beginning of the 13th century. In those of the choir is a double row of figures representing the ancestors of Christ, and scenes from the Old Testament (about 1180). One of the finest depicts a monumental and expressive figure of Methuselah, his elbow resting on his knee, stroking his beard with his hand. The principal colours are red and blue, luminous brown and a little yellow and green. In the aisles of the same choir are twelve stained glass windows with theological scenes linking up the Old Testament with the New. In the Chapel of the Holy Trinity is a series depicting miracles, and the *Life and Martyrdom of Thomas Becket*.

Chartres (France)

Under the rose window on the façade are three remarkable windows which escaped the fire of 1194. They illustrate *The Last Judgement* and date from the 12th century (1150). They are the work of the St. Denis school of glass workers. *The Tree of Jesse* is similar to the one of that basilica (of which we have a few fragments). *The Infancy of Christ* is portrayed in twenty-nine medallions. St. Joseph wears a Phrygian cap similar to the one worn by Moses in a stained glass window at St. Denis. Here again we find circular and square medallions used together, and the red star-spangled border, so characteristic of Dionysian art. The third stained glass window depicts the fourteen scenes of the Passion. In the ambulatory on the right near the south transept is a fine stained glass window known as *Notre-Dame-de-la-Belle-*

Verrière which, although of a later period (1180), is still Romanesque in style.

Cîteaux (France)

The celebrated Burgundian Abbey, seat of the Cistercian order, a branch of the Benedictines. It was founded in the diocese of Langres in 1098, by St. Robert, Abbot of Solesme, in a place which, owing to its natural reservoirs, was named Cîteaux. The new monastery was elevated to the status of an abbey by the Bishop of Châlons. Robert, however, could not stay long as head of his new abbey; he had to return to Solesme, leaving a new prior, St. Alberic, in charge. Alberic obtained confirmation of his order in 1100. He placed his monks under the "Old Rule of St. Benedict", and gave them white habits as a sign of special devotion to the Virgin. When he died in 1109, he was succeeded by the Englishman Stephen Harding, to whom St. Bernard and thirty of his companions came in 1113, asking to take the habit. From then on, Cîteaux grew rapidly. Monks came in such numbers that it was necessary to found new colonies outside. The Abbeys of La Ferté, Pontigny, Clairvaux and Morimont grew up within three years; they were the first four "daughters" of Cîteaux, which was later to have so many more. Some manuscripts notable for their very sober ornamentation, illuminated by the monks of Cîteaux, have come down to us.

Engolasters (Valley of Andorra)

The paintings in the apse of San Miguel at Engolasters (Barcelona Museum) show a *Christ Pantocrator* in the vault. Above are two angels carrying the lion of St. Mark and the bull of St. Luke in medallions; to the left of Christ is a great eagle symbolising St. John. St. Matthew is represented on the right of the Saviour by St. Michael, patron of the church. The Archangel holds a standard, the staff of which, like a lance, transfixes the dragon at his feet. On the lower portion of the cylindrical wall are seated apostles, holding scrolls, with the exception of St. Peter, who bears the keys. At the summit of the soffit of the triumphal arch: the Agnus Dei upheld by the Elect. Above are the busts of those apostles who are absent from the interior. The new methods introduced by the master of Urgel may be seen in these frescoes, and they have been attributed to one of his pupils, the master of Santa Coloma. They date from the second half of the 12th century.

Ferentillo (Italy)

The paintings in the Abbey church of St. Peter at Ferentillo near Terni consist of three registers on each wall. On the left-hand wall are scenes from the Old Testament and on the right from the New. A number of the paintings have been damaged, but others are in a good state of repair: especially the *Creation of the World*, the *Creation of Adam*, *Adam Naming the Animals*, and *The Creation of Eve*. There are also the stories of Cain and Abel, Noah, Abraham and Isaac. High up on the right-hand wall Christ is represented in a mandorla between prophets and angels. Also depicted is the Infancy of Christ with an *Adoration of the Magi* in very good repair. Beneath this the story continues from the *Entry into Jerusalem* up to *Calvary*. These frescoes date from the last quarter of the 12th century.

Gargilesse (France)

This village in the Indre possesses a magnificent Romanesque church of the 12th century. It is a building with three aisles, with strangely decorated capitals, and beneath, a crypt also with three aisles (containing a statue of the Virgin of the 12th century and some Gothic paintings). A remarkable Romanesque stained glass window representing *Christ in Glory* has survived.

Germigny-des-Prés (France)

Bishop Theodulf of Orleans, a friend of Charlemagne, erected in 806 a church attached to his villa at Germigny-des-Prés. The vault of the apse is decorated with a mosaic of the 9th century. It represents the Ark of the Covenant surmounted by cherubim. The decoration of Solomon's temple as described in the Bible is reproduced. Standing among exotic plants, the Ark is presented as the focal point of the sanctuary, the ideal temple which rises in the middle of a sort of Paradise and is the perfect symbol of Jehovah. Beneath the ark and the propitiatory cherubim are two immense angels who point upwards to the Ark. Their bodies outline the arch of the apse and the tips of their spread wings are interlaced. Below, a Latin inscription explains the subject.

Gotland, Island of (Sweden)

The frescoes of the churches on the island of Gotland are less retouched than other Romanesque ones in Sweden. A strong Byzantine influence is evident. At Källunge and Havden only fragments survive. The church of Garda still has figures of several saints on the vault of the bell tower. Their garments are richly ornamented, the hands in characteristic poses and the faces strongly modelled, with shadowed eyes.

Hix (Valley of Andorra)

The altar frontal of Hix (middle of the 12th century) is one of the masterpieces of Catalan painting on wood. The technique of painting is egg tempera applied to a panel coated with glue. It is possible that the frontal at Hix is by the hand of the master of Urgel himself. The figures and the garments with their rich borders are worked in his style. Particularly remarkable is the scene where St. Martin divides his cloak and gives half to a beggar. The colours are fresh and startling, and the figures, outlined with black, of great hieratic power. The expression of the faces is noble and of an almost primitive strength (Barcelona Museum).

Le Mans (France)

The Romanesque stained glass of the Cathedral, set in windows of the same period, lights up the aisles of the nave. The subjects are: the *Legend of St. Gervais and St. Protais* (which show a common origin with those of Chartres); the *Legend of St. Stephen*, equally a work of artist glass workers from Chartres; the *Story of St. Julian*, the panels of which, according to Emile Mâle, should be attributed to a local artist owing to the heaviness of the design. In the southern aisle is the famous window of the *Ascension*. It shows the Virgin surrounded by a group of apostles gazing up to heaven. The panel in which Christ is shown flanked by two angels and ascending to heaven is the only modern work. This window was long considered as belonging to the 11th century and was looked upon as the most ancient specimen of stained glass in Europe. Modern critics hold this to be quite untrue. All the characteristics of this window, and of the panes of the other cycles, is typical of the 12th century stained glass—as practised by the glass workers of St. Denis.

Le Puy (Auvergne)

The Chapel of Saint Michel d'Aiguilhe. In the vault of the choir: a Christ in Majesty and the Archangel Michael between two seraphim. These figures stand within a circular glory. At the four corners are the symbols of the Evangelists. This work, which dates from the 10th century, is seriously damaged, and the colours have unfortunately been retouched. The composition of the group is reminiscent of Carolingian work. The almost effaced paintings on the walls date from the end of the Romanesque and the beginning of the Gothic periods.

The Cathedral. The north gallery of the transept contains the most important group of early Romanesque frescoes (11th century) surviving in France. The figure of St. Michael, 5½ metres in height, is the largest painted figure existing in the country. He is dressed in Byzantine robes with the scarf, called the *loros*, set with plaques of gold and precious stones. A hieratic figure, he transfixes the dragon with his lance, without even glancing at it. Amongst the less effaced scenes are a *Judgement of Solomon*, a figure of St. Paul, some peacocks, scenes of martyrdom, and geometrical and floral designs. The chapel of St. Martin contains a recently discovered group of the 12th century: Christ and the Virgin in Majesty, animals and foliage. The frescoes in the chapels of the northern arm of the transept date from the end of the 12th century. On the right is the *Martyrdom of St. Catherine*; and on the left the *Holy Women at the Tomb*. High up in the chapter house, on facing walls are two curious frescoes, one representing a game of chess between a Moorish king and Charlemagne, the other the siege of a town by the Crusaders (middle of the 12th century). Also in the chapter house is a *Crucifixion*, framed by four figures: three prophets, and the philosopher Philo (early 13th century). This is a transitional work with some similarity to those at Rocamadour (the same blue star-spangled background and the same static effect borrowed from the figures in stained glass).

Montmorillon (Poitou)

A group of frescoes of the late 12th century is in the crypt of the church of Notre-Dame. *The Mystic Marriage of St. Catherine*, in which the saint is wearing the ring which Jesus has just given her. The latter is on the lap of his Mother, surrounded by a mandorla. Around are much effaced scenes from the *Life of St. Catherine*. In front of the ceiling beam two fine figures of the *Elders of the Apocalypse* have survived. The elegance and grace of these paintings show a spirit that is already Gothic. Only the elders above have retained the epic grandeur and sobriety of the Romanesque age.

Müstair (Grisons)

The Abbey church of the convent at Müstair possesses a remarkable group of frescoes of the Carolingian period, but they have been spoiled by restorations. Certain parts, also, such as *The Ascension* and various other scenes have been removed and are now in the Landesmuseum in Zurich. Particularly interesting are: the *Scenes of St. John the Baptist, St. Peter, St. Paul* and *St. Stephen:* the cycle of events from the Old Testament and the Gospels (in all, eighty-two episodes divided into rectangles, all of the same size); and above the entrance, a large *Last Judgement*. The heads are somewhat monotonous, the features all alike, but the attitudes are animated. A certain stylisation is the precursor of Ottonian art. The scenes are set in very varied architectural and decorative backgrounds. Aesthetically Müstair belongs to the period of antique painting, though traces of Byzantine influence can also be seen.

Naturno (Italian Tyrol)

The church of St. Proculo possesses a few fragments of painting from the 9th century, the best preserved of which is *St. Paul Fleeing from Damascus*. The outline stands out on a white background. The artist has undoubtedly been influenced by Hiberno-Saxon manuscripts.

Neuwiller (France)

The stained glass window depicting *St. Timothy* from Neuwiller (Bas-Rhin) dates from the second half of the 12th century. It is now in the Cluny Museum. Its characteristics, both iconographical and technical, class it among the group of stained glass from Champagne.

Osormort (Catalonia)

The surviving paintings in the apse of the church of St. Saturnino (now in the Episcopal Museum at Vich) are the remains of a *Virgin and Child* (much effaced) in a mandorla (in the vaulting), and two wide bands which divide the semi-circular apse wall. Above are the twelve apostles standing in a meadow, in animated discussion. The lower portion shows various scenes from the beginning of Genesis: the creation of Adam, his introduction into Paradise, the Original Sin, God reprimanding Adam and Eve for their sin, and their expulsion from the Garden—decorated with beautiful floral motifs on a dark background. The painter of these also worked in the churches of El Brull and Bellcaire. He is easily recognisable by his narrative skill, by the archaic style of his nudes, and his research into naturalism, notably in the folds of the garments which are draped in the most simple manner. His colours are sober—white wash, blue, ochre, red ochre and a natural green. The style of his work is very similar to that of the Italo-Byzantine murals and especially to that of the French artists from the region of Poitou. It is possible that he was a pupil of the master of St. Savin-sur-Gartempe. Many parallels can be drawn between the decoration of this crypt and the work of the master of Osormort.

Ottonian (Art and Renaissance)

In the 10th century, thanks to the Ottonian Emperors of the house of Saxony, Germany had become a great power. This resulted in a brilliant cultural and artistic Renaissance, which took the name of the dynasty. The founder of this line, Otto I the Great (910-973), regarded himself as the restorer of the Frankish Empire and did his best to emulate Charlemagne. He wished to reinstate that intellectual culture which had contributed so much to the glory of his model. He received hospitably the Irish and Anglo-Saxon monks fleeing from the Norsemen. He had married an Anglo-Saxon princess himself, the pious Edith, daughter of King Edward. When she died in 946, he learned to read so that he could study the Bible. His brother Bruno (925-966) was brought up in the schools of Lorraine under the care of Balderic, Bishop of Utrecht, and became one of the most scholarly men of the period. He knew Greek, and the classics as well as ecclesiastical literature. He reorganised the discipline of the Church and the schools. Otto made him Arch-chaplain and Chancellor of the kingdom. With the help of the Irish monks, he propagated the rule of St. Benedict. He re-established the palace school, and to the trivium (grammar, rhetoric and dialectic) he added the quadrivium of higher sciences (mathematics, geometry, music and astronomy). From Lorraine and Italy, he summoned teachers, Rutherius of Verona and Bishop Luitprand of Cremona. He bought manuscripts of the classics from Italy; in the palace school, Cicero, Sallust, Virgil, Ovid and Horace were studied. This impetus was felt no less in architecture and painting. Particularly remarkable are the illuminated manuscripts of the Ottonian period, of which Reichenau was one of the principal producers.

Poitiers (Poitou)

The Baptistry of St. John. The decoration is of the 12th century, the colours of which are much faded. On the upper part of the west wall are an *Ascension of Christ*, between two angels, and *The Apostles* divided into two groups. The legs of one of the apostles are crossed, which shows the influence of the Languedoc school of sculpture. On the east and west walls are four remarkable figures of crowned knights. It seems that these are equestrian effigies of Christian Emperors—Constantine, Constant, Theodosius and Valentinian II. On the north wall are two saints surrounded by monsters and peacocks. The upper frieze is decorated with a Greek key pattern and squares enclosing birds, which show the influence of Gallo-Roman mosaics. The painting itself resembles that in St. Savin; but there is something more supple in the drawing of the equestrian figures.

Notre-Dame-la-Grande. The vaulting in the choir still has all its painted decoration, but is, as a whole, sadly effaced. In the summit are: the Virgin in Majesty holding the Child in her lap; Christ in Majesty, enclosed in two mandorlas; four angels supporting a medallion containing the Lamb. On the sides of the vaulting are apostles and various figures. The influence of St. Savin is easily recognisable in these frescoes which date from the 12th century. In the crypt are some well preserved murals of the 11th century. In the vaulting are: Christ in Majesty, the Lamb and the symbols of the Evangelists in medallions. On

the walls are two life-sized and two half-sized figures, and remarkable stylised decorations. The range of colours is restrained but the figures which resemble those of icons are very clearly drawn.

St. Hilaire-le-Grand. This church was entirely frescoed, but the murals are not yet quite free from the whitewash that covered them. Visible are: (a) in the roof of the transept, a finely decorated frieze, and beneath the bell-tower, a portrait of a 9th century benefactor; (b) on four pillars in the nave, groups of figures, much elongated, from the end of the 11th century; (c) in the chapels of the apse five large panels, probably representing scenes from the life of St. Hilary (second half of the 12th century).

At the east end of the Cathedral is a remarkable 12th century, stained glass window. On a blue background, red panels are inset, representing *The Crucifixion*, *The Ascension*, *The Resurrection* and *The Martyrdom of St. Peter*. The influence of the painter-glass workers of St. Denis is clear. The apostles in the *Ascension* resemble those at Le Mans. The square medallion in which *The Crucifixion of St. Peter* is depicted is decorated with a cruciform design as in *The Ascension* at Le Mans and in the stained glass *Virgin* at Vendôme.

Prüfening (Germany)

The frescoes in the Cluniac Abbey of Prüfening date from about 1150, the work of painters from the studio of Ratisbon. Byzantine influence is noticeable. In the choir is a *Celestial Jerusalem:* above a Christ surrounded by apostles. In the vaulting is the Church personified, around it a host of saints arranged in four registers. At the base of the walls on the sides are portraits of the donors, *Bishop Otto of Bamberg* and the *Emperor Henry V.* Decorative difficulties have induced the artist to attempt a *trompe-l'œil* of veined and coloured marble flagstones. In the north chapel is the *Story of St. John the Baptist* with a *Celestial Jerusalem* in the vaulting; and in the vaulting of the south chapel the *Life of St. Benedict*, with a dove, symbol of the Holy Ghost, descending on the apostles.

Rheims (France)

Rheims was the capital of the Rémi, a Gallo-Belgian tribe. Its bishopric was created about 290 by St. Sixtus; but its religious organisation did not develop fully until the pontificate of St. Nicaise, who on the site of the present Cathedral erected a church in about 400. It was on the steps of this church that he was martyred by the Vandals in 406. Amongst his immediate successors may be mentioned St. Rémi, the illustrious prelate whose episcopacy lasted seventy-four years (459-533). He succeeded in converting Clovis and baptised him solemnly on Christmas Day 496 in the Cathedral built by St. Nicaise. It was to commemorate this baptism that the kings of France adopted the custom of being crowned at Rheims. During the Carolingian period, the town became a cultural centre. Its remarkable school of illuminators popularised a style that was realist and dynamic. It played an important role in the development of Romanesque art in the North of France, England and all the countries of North-West Europe. For several centuries the illuminators drew their inspiration from the essential discoveries of this school. The illuminations in the Gospels of Elbo, which date from the 9th century, clearly reveal this influence. The stained glass windows in the church of St. Rémi date from the end of the 12th century, and have been restored at various times. They have since been mounted on borders of grisaille, having originally filled smaller windows.

The suppleness of the draperies and the plasticity of the modelling are forerunners of Gothic art.

Rocamadour

On a rock outside the chapel of St. Michael is a Romanesque fresco which, owing to being protected by an overhang from the mountain, is in an exceptional state of preservation. The colours are remarkably fresh. Two scenes are represented: *The Annunciation* and *The Visitation*. They date from the end of the 12th century. They are deftly executed, but the figures have the immobility of stained glass. This quality, together with the decoration of the background (a crude blue, spangled with stars) indicates that it is a transitional work.

St. Denis (Paris)

The surviving stained glass windows in St. Denis are those that Suger, the builder of the basilica ordered between 1144, the date of the dedication of the choir, and 1151 when he died. Unfortunately only a very small part of the whole remains. Viollet-le-Duc had them framed in a modern surround. They represent: The Tree of Jesse (incomplete), decorative gryphons, episodes from the story of Moses and allegorical scenes. One of them depicts Christ. From His breast spread seven doves (the seven gifts of the Holy Spirit). With one hand He crowns the personification of the Church, and with the other unveils the face of the Synagogue. The explanatory legend reads "That which Moses veiled, Christ reveals". The other shows the four-horsed chariot of Aminadab or the triumphal chariot of the Song of Songs. The four symbols of the Evangelists are placed close to the four wheels, to show that they provide the motive power for the chariot. In this sort of biblical Ark the Tables of the Law and Aaron's Rod are depicted. Above stands a green cross, on which is a figure of Christ Crucified, upheld by God the Father. Like the preceding window, this is dedicated to the concordance between the Old and New Testaments. The sureness of the composition and the colour technique are admirable.

St. Jacques-des-Guérets
(Valley of the Loire)

The most important group of frescoes in the Loire valley; some scenes have unfortunately been retouched, especially the faces. Two paintings survive on the north wall of the nave: *The Nativity*, where the Virgin is lying on a bed, whilst the Child is resting on an altar supported by a column; and the *Massacre of the Innocents*, treated with originality and tenderness. In the choir to the left of the central window are: a *Crucifixion* where the cross is worked like a piece of jewellery, whilst the sun and the moon, placed on either side, are given the faces of a man and a woman; the *Resurrection of the Dead* where the sarcophagi are of a much earlier type than the time when these frescoes were painted. To the right of the window stands the traditional figure of Christ in Majesty, in very striking colours. Beneath is the *Last Supper*, in a cruder style. In the embrasures of the same window are the figures of *St. George* and *St. Augustine*. On the right-hand wall on either side of the next window are: *Pride*, depicted as a rider thrown by his horse; *Despair*, transfixed by his own sword. Above is the *Martyrdom of St. James the Great*, remarkable for its composition and colouring. A little farther on, in the upper section, is an episode taken from the legend of St. Nicholas: the saint is throwing gold pieces into a room where three young girls are sleeping. Their

father, on account of his poverty, is about to sell them into a life of debauchery; the saint saves them from dishonour and sin. In the lower section is the *Raising of Lazarus*, with well balanced groups of figures. The next scene, divided into three levels, is the *Descent of Christ into Limbo*. The Christ is particularly majestic and the struggle between the damned and the infernal monsters very realistic.

St. Savin-sur-Gartempe (Poitou)

The church contains one of the finest remaining groups of murals of the 12th century. It is due to Prosper Mérimée, then inspector of historical monuments, that these frescoes were discovered and made known in 1845. *The Porch*. The frescoes, in many places effaced, have the Apocalypse of St. John as their subject. On the tympanum, God appears in the Celestial Jerusalem, accompanied by twelve angels who point to gates of which the twelve apostles are the foundation. Among the best preserved visions are: the *Plague of Locusts* (at the top of the north vault); *The Four Angels released and the Beast* (south side); *The Woman attacked by the Beast* (north side); and *The New Jerusalem* (the farthest side). The style resembles that of the illuminated manuscripts from St. Martial of Limoges with its particular stylisation (due to a combination of indigenous tendencies and southern influence and its dynamic power).
Gallery. The frescoes here are very faded, but a fine *Descent from the Cross* very much in the Byzantine tradition can be seen in the tympanum. On the east wall is *Christ between the Virgin and St. John*. At the summit of the eastern arch appear two angels holding out a starry disc on which a cross is painted. *The Hanging of Judas* (on the southern arcade) is beneath *The Holy Women at the Tomb*; in the east bay: three apostles and St. Savin arrested by

soldiers; on the pilasters: portraits of the holy bishops of Poitiers. Here, unlike the figures in the porch, the style is static and architectural.

Nave. In the vaulting a great biblical cycle comprises: *The Creation* with the story of Adam and Eve and their children up to the curse of Jehovah on Cain and the ascension of Enoch, the story of Noah, the Tower of Babel, story of Abraham and of Joseph, and of Moses up to the presentation of the Tables of the Law. The cycle is unfolded on four bands which extend from the west gallery to the transept. A decorative border of foliage between two rows of pearls outlines the barrel vault from one end of the nave to the other. Romanesque art here attains one of its highest points of perfection: a perfect animation of the figures, the drawing both supple and vigorous, well balanced composition and bright colours.

The Crypt. Christ in Majesty is above the altar, and there are numerous episodes from the lives of SS. Savin and Cyprien. Amongst the more remarkable are Savin and Cyprien exhorting the people of Amphipolis; the executioners tearing the flesh of the martyrs with iron pincers; the two saints in the furnace; and the saints thrown to the lions. The workmanship of these paintings is very different from others in the same church: the figures are more squat and appear to be inspired from manuscripts, and the colours are cruder. These proportions and the quality of the colouring are explained by the necessity to conform to the lowness of the vaulting and the dimness of the light.

San Bastianello (Italy)

The small church of San Bastianello, on the Palatine in Rome, was given by Pope Alexander II to Desiderius, Abbot of Monte Cassino. In the shell of the apse, stands a Christ pointing to a phoenix, symbol of the Resurrection, perched on a palm tree. Above the Saviour appears the hand of God and at His sides are St. Zoticus, St. Sebastian, St. Lawrence and St. Stephen. Lower down the Holy Lamb stands on a hillock, surrounded by twelve lambs, the apostles, who are emerging from two small buildings representing Bethlehem and Jerusalem. In the lower part the Virgin is seen surrounded by two archangels, four martyrs, and St. Benedict between SS. Peter and Sebastian.

San Biagio (Italy)

The grotto of St. Biagio near Castellamare contains a *Christ with a cruciform halo*, between the Alpha and the Omega. His hair and beard are black, His features regular and His expression calm. Beside Him are the Archangels Michael and Gabriel and two aged apostles, thin with long grey beards. The treatment of these pictures is rather conventional and resembles some of the Benedictine illuminations. A different type of Christ, more finely executed and with a more humanised expression, is represented between the busts of two men and two archangels which resemble the figures in the Romano-Byzantine mosaics of the 9th century. Amongst other paintings in this grotto are: *St. Finniabus*, her face pale and emaciated, carrying a jewelled crown; a *Virgin and Child* between St. John the Baptist, with a Latin inscription, and St. Peter holding the keys (the details are completely Western, as is the Virgin's crown). These frescoes date from the 11th century.

San Clemente (Rome)

In the underground church of San Clemente in Rome are frescoes illustrating the lives of St. Clement and St. Alexis. They were probably done during the Pontificate of Gregory VII, whose reign began in 1073, and certainly before 1084, when the church was abandoned. These scenes, comprising a quantity of priests and laymen in contemporary 11th century costumes have great vivacity and charm. The faces are treated delicately, with finely modelled contours. Both subtle and realistic, they are painted in white, red and ochre, a technique recalling that of certain contemporary illuminated manuscripts.

San Vincenzo-al-Volturno (Italy)

The frescoes in the chapel of the crypt of St. Vincent, at the source of the Volturno, were painted between 826 and 843. They consist of six female saints, dressed in the robes of Greek princesses, separated into two groups by a vase. They wear jewelled diadems and appear to be advancing towards the centre of the chapel where the *Virgin* is enthroned, surrounded by angels. There follow two scenes: *The Martyrdom of St. Lawrence* lying on his grid whilst two executioners hold him there with forks; and the *Martyrdom of St. Stephen. Christ in Majesty* fills the opposite vault. He has a cruciform halo and stands upon a half-globe, blessing in the Greek manner. Beside Him stand St. Lawrence and St. Stephen. On either side are depicted the *Annunciation*, *The Baptism of Christ*, *The Crucifixion* and *The Holy Women at the Tomb*. A figure of the Virgin completes the series. She is clad in royal robes and seated on a throne, within a circular mandorla. She holds on her lap an oval frame in which is Jesus giving benediction in the Greek manner and holding a scroll in His left hand. At the feet of Mary kneels Abbot Epiphanius.

Santa Coloma (Valley of Andorra)

The frescoes of this little church have been transferred to the walls of Baron de Cassel's house at Cannes. The painter, who has been called the master of Santa Coloma, managed to produce an extraordinary sense of rhythm considering the problem he had to face in decorating a square chapel with a barrel vault and flat walls. The vault is divided longitudinally into two sections by a border of foliage. On the left is the Christ Pantocrator surrounded by the symbols of the four Evangelists; on the right are six apostles surmounted by a painted arcade. On the wall of the chancel on a similar arcade are: the Virgin and St. Coloma, the apostles Peter and Paul on either side of a window above which hovers the dove of the Holy Ghost. In the interior decoration of the triumphal arch are two haloed saints; on the intrados St. Gervais and St. Protais; and on its exterior face the Agnus Dei presented by two angels (this motif alone remains *in situ*). The lower part is painted with hangings on which are medallions of figures and mythological animals. The master of Santa Coloma was a disciple of the master of Urgel.

Sant' Angelo in Formis (Italy)

In the tympanum of the narthex stands the *Archangel Michael* in imperial robes holding the sceptre and the orb, a typically Byzantine figure. Above is the *Virgin-Queen*, in prayer, her arms widespread, within a medallion supported by flying angels. The inscriptions are in Greek. The external wall of the façade has four episodes from the story of the hermits, Anthony and Paul, subject borrowed from the legend of the Egyptian monks, very popular in the East. In the interior, the entrance wall is entirely covered by a big painting of the *Last Judgement* with on either side scenes from the Old Testament: the story of Adam and Eve, Noah's Ark, and the judgement of a martyr, etc. There is also a series of medallions containing the portraits of the abbots of Monte Cassino. In the north aisle are other scenes from the Old Testament. They include the stories of Abraham, Jacob and Noah. On the walls of the nave above the pillars are the figures of Amos, Daniel, Sophonia, Hosea, Solomon, David, the Persian Sybil, Moses, Zachariah, Malachi, Balaam, Micah, Jeremiah, Ezekiel and Isaiah. Scenes from the life of Christ decorate the upper portions of the nave; among those that survive are: *The Magi before Herod*, *The Massacre of the Innocents*, *Jesus teaching in the Temple*, *The Sermon of St. John*, *The Baptism of Christ*, *The Sermon on the Mount*, *the Feast of Lazarus*, *Christ visiting Zachariah*, *Christ and the Woman taken in Adultery*, *The Entry into Jerusalem*, *The Last Supper*, *The Garden of Olives*, *The Crucifixion*, and *The Descent into Limbo*. The apse is decorated with a painting, mainly in the Byzantine style, similar to those in the narthex; Christ seated on a jewelled throne, holding a book with a Latin inscription, is the central theme. Above his head is the dove of the Holy Ghost and around him are the symbols of the four Evangelists. Below are three angels, St. Benedict holding the Rules of his Order and Abbot Desiderius, in a rectangular halo, bearing a model of the church in his hands. In the side apses are a *Madonna and Child* surrounded by archangels, and some figures of saints. The frescoes in the narthex must have been done by a Greek artist, but those in the nave and apse are a mixture of Byzantine and Italic style. They are surely the works of native painters.

Sant' Urbano alla Caffarella (Rome)

Facing the entrance of this little church not far from the Via Appia, there is a Christ giving the blessing and holding the Gospels, flanked by St. Peter, St. Paul and two angels. The style of the Saviour, his manner of blessing, as well as the absence of the keys in the hands of St. Peter and of the sword in those of St. Paul, show a Byzantine influence. The Crucifixion above the door has been repainted, its main interest being that it is dated 1011. It is the centre of a series of eighteen episodes in the life of Christ from the Annunciation to the descent into Limbo and a *Noli me tangere*. There are also some scenes of martyrdom, St. Urban, St. Cecilia and St. Lawrence. These works are full of animation and realism. The figures express strongly the most diverse feelings. The frescoes in this church are a good example of the narrative style of Romanesque art.

Santi Stefani (Italy)

The grotto of Santi Stefani near Vasto, in the province of Otranto, contains a number of paintings, now very damaged, which date from various centuries. The majority are of the 14th century and depict saints. Many are in the Western style, for example, *St. Francis* and *St. Anthony with his pig*; only a few details sometimes show an Eastern influence. These frescoes are dated 1376, but mostly have been repainted. A *Madonna and Child* in a niche and a number of saints on the pillars are of the same date. A *St. Philip*, however, is older and can be attributed to the 12th century, to which also belong other frescoes in this grotto including a *Christ*, His face refined and calm, between two deeply inclined angels; a *St. Nicholas* and a *St. Basil* each holding a book: *St. Gregory of Nazianzus* with a cross, and a fine *St. Michael*, clad in red and blue. All these figures are of a completely oriental type and the inscriptions are in Greek.

Schwarzrheindorf (Germany)

The paintings in the crypt were covered over in the 16th century, covered again with whitewash in 1846, and later uncovered, restored and "completed". Thus their original character and colour can no longer be discerned. *The Pantocrator* might well be a work of the 19th century; but the *Cycle of Ezekiel* conforms approximately to the spirit of the period in which it was painted. It unfolds in twenty episodes, divided among the five ribbed vaults. Every possible inch of space is decorated, and the series is rich in dramatic scenes which are forceful and expressive. They are taken from the book of Ezekiel, the prophet who foretold the Babylonian captivity, the fall of Jerusalem and its rebuilding. Amongst the more remarkable paintings are: *Ezekiel in Ecstasy* (near him one of those wheels of fire of which he speaks in his prophecies); *Ezekiel among the Ancient Prophets*; *Ezekiel showing the Jews how to serve God*; *Ezekiel cutting off his Beard and Hair with a Sword*; and *The Punishment of Jerusalem*.

Tahull (Catalonia)

The church of St. Clement. The church used to be entirely covered with frescoes. Only those of the central apse and of one of the smaller apses remain. In the vaulting is the *Pantocrator* in a large mandorla. He is seated on a curved frieze decorated with foliage on a blue background. His mantle and tunic are pleated in a most realistic manner; the hands are delicately modelled, and the elongated face has an impressive serenity. Three horizontal bands of blue, ochre and dark grey divide the rest of the vault, in which four angels bear the symbols of the Evangelists. Two are in the upper part. One without the usual symbol alludes to St. Matthew; the other bears the Eagle of St. John. In the lower part the others are represented half-size in medallions. Beside them, also in medallions, are the lion of St. Mark and the bull of St. Luke. The angels hold these animals, one by the paw, the other by the tail, in an attitude which is full of naïve and

natural grace. Two seraphim whose six wings are decorated with eyes complete the composition. On the apse wall, five apostles and the Virgin stand out against a background half-blue, half-red in a blind arcade. The strangely elongated face of the Virgin is stylised, but it radiates an intense and mysterious spiritual quality. She is holding the Holy Grail from which flames seem to be darting. On the keystone of the triumphal arch is the Lamb of the Apocalypse with seven eyes; on the keystone of the other arch a majestic hand of God. This is all that remains, except for the figure of the Patriarch Jacob and a remarkably drawn *Lazarus* before the gate of the wicked rich man, accompanied by a dog which is licking his sores. The outstanding artist who painted these works has employed the Byzantine formula, while impressing on it his own particular vigour and rhythm. The life-like quality is combined with a feeling of hieratic grandeur, giving the figures great expressive force.

The small apse, in which only six angels separated by bands of various colours remain, was painted by another artist. The latter was also responsible for the decoration of the lateral walls of the church of St. Mary.

The Church of St. Mary. The apse vaulting is decorated with the *Epiphany* (Barcelona Museum). The background is composed of horizontal bands of blue, green, ochre and black. An immense figure of the Virgin is seated on a jewelled throne within a mandorla. The Child on her lap is giving the blessing with his right hand. On the right of the Virgin is Melchior, and on the left Caspar and Balthazar. The three kings are bearing their offerings on golden platters. A meander pattern is depicted at the juncture of the lower part of the vaulting and the apse wall. Upon the latter are the apostles (only Peter, Paul and John have survived) who stand out on a background of parallel coloured bands framed in a richly decorated blind arcade. On the arch the *Agnus Dei* is on the keystone, flanked by Cain and Abel (now effaced). Of the decoration of the choir, only an angel with the head of a bull and another with the head of an eagle, symbols of St. Luke and St. John, have survived, together with a seraph and the Archangel Gabriel. The painter of these frescoes belonged to the same school as the one who painted in St. Clement's; but he had not the genius of the former. He had less talent and was incapable of giving freshness to the traditional formulas. Nevertheless his figures are full of expression and serenity.

Tarrasa (Catalonia)

The remaining decoration, still in place, of the small apse of the transept in the church of St. Mary is given a special interest by a scene from contemporary history. It is dedicated to St. Thomas of Canterbury, who was murdered in 1170, and canonised three years later. On the exterior of the entrance arch are a series of circles, and on the keystone an angel carrying a much damaged nimbus, in the centre of which was possibly the Virgin or the soul of St. Thomas. In the vaulting, the Pantocrator is seated on a cushioned throne, in a mandorla, with a background of stars. In either hand he carries an open book resting on the heads of St. Thomas and his deacon, Edward Grim. The two priests are standing close to the Saviour on a background of coloured bands, on which are set the seven-branched candlesticks of the Apocalypse. A frieze with incomplete inscriptions separates the vaulting from the apse wall. On the latter the life of the saint is depicted with no division between individual scenes. To the right three soldiers are attacking Thomas and his deacon, a scene followed by the beheading of the martyr and his burial.

The soul of the holy bishop is being borne up to heaven by two angels.

Tavant (Poitou)

Crypt. The crypt of Tavant, which is gloomy and constricted, is divided into three aisles by two rows of pillars. It is completely frescoed: the shafts of the pillars, with rose-coloured plaster, are dappled white, and the walls and vaultings whitewashed. The groins of the vault are emphasised by broad strokes of carmine edged with yellow. On the small arches of the pillars are characters who appear connected in some symbolic but obscure way. In the central nave, facing one another, are: two saints, two angels holding a candlestick, *Adam and Eve before the Tree of Good and Evil*, around which is coiled the serpent; *Saul* with, opposite, *David playing the Harp*; two persons who appear to be supporting the vault; *Lust*; *Sagittarius*; *David slaying a Lion with the Sword*; a Virtue in a coat of mail and crushing a Vice; Adam delving while Eve spins; a *Mater Dolorosa*; a *Descent from the Cross*; *Christ in Limbo*; *The Crucifixion of St. Peter*; and *The Sacrifice of Cain and Abel*. On the back wall is the figure of *Christ in Majesty*. These frescoes date from the first half of the 12th century.

Winchester

The most interesting frescoes are in the Chapel of the Holy Sepulchre. In the vaulting, in medallions, are a Christ with the symbols of the Evangelists, *The Annunciation*, *The Nativity* and the *Annunciation to the Shepherds*. On the east wall, beneath a half-figure of Christ on the vault, a *Descent from the Cross* and an *Entombment*; on the other walls, *The Entry into Jerusalem* and a *Noli me tangere*. These paintings date from about 1230.